MW01633878

Baseball

GAME INTELLIGENCE

IQ

The Difference-Maker in Umpiring

By Matt Moore

FROM *REFEREE* MAGAZINE & THE NATIONAL ASSOCIATION OF SPORTS OFFICIALS

Baseball Game Intelligence: The Difference-Maker in Umpiring

By Matt Moore

Cover and layout by Matt Bowen, graphic designer, *Referee* magazine

Copyright © 2011 by Referee Enterprises, Inc.

Copying in whole or in part is prohibited without prior written consent from Referee Enterprises, Inc. Republication of all or any part of this publication, including on the Internet, is expressly prohibited.

Published by Referee Enterprises, Inc., and the National Association of Sports Officials.

Printed in the United States of America

ISBN-13: 978-1-58208-177-9

TABLE OF CONTENTS

INTRODUCTION

There are three main areas that umpires must master in order to be successful.

A successful umpire must have a mastery of the rules in order to handle the plays and problems that happen on the field.

Additionally, the successful umpire must know the proper mechanics that are appropriate for the game being worked.

Third, an umpire must adapt a philosophy in step with today's game. The days are gone where umpires can run roughshod over players, coaches and the game itself. An umpire must be in tune with the prevailing philosophy of each game's keepers — that includes the players, coaches, umpire supervisor, league or conference officials, governing body and more.

There are plenty of books on the market that are designed to improve rules and mechanics knowledge. Those are not the goal of this book; instead I hope that it will provide you with a fresh look at the philosophies in umpiring and in turn, improve your game intelligence. Armed with more game intelligence, you will be better able to deal with the responsibilities, expectations and scrutiny that today's umpire must handle to be successful.

Between the covers of this book you will find chapters that deal with such matters as pregame musts, the most important thing in umpiring, working with your crew, assignments, annual clinics and postgame discussion.

A number of skilled writers and talented officials contributed to this book. They are Jon Bible, a former Division I conference coordinator who worked six College World Series; George Demetriou, a veteran high school umpire and rules interpreter; Mike Droll, an umpire in the Big 10 and Big 12 conferences and veteran of several NCAA postseason tournaments; Jason Smith, a former high school and college umpire from Florida; Rick Woelfel, a freelance writer and umpire from Philadelphia; Dave Yeast, the former NCAA coordinator of baseball umpires and myself.

I hope you find the book meets its goal — to provide you with useful information that improves your game intelligence and takes your umpiring to the next level.

Matt Moore
Associate editor
Referee magazine

CHAPTER

TOPICS THAT MUST BE COVERED EVERY PREGAME

In an ideal world, an umpire crew would convene before every game or series in ample time to do a thorough pregame covering all aspects of mechanics, handling situations and arguments, non-verbal signals, checked-swing and swipe-tag responsibilities, etc.

Each member would have a copy of the pregame outline that applies at his level — CCA guide in college ball, NFHS guide in high school, etc. — and they would run through it item by item. The reality, however, is that often does not happen. Perhaps the crewmates have worked together for many years and don't see the need for an A-to-Z review. Possibly some member(s) waited until the last second to leave work and had to race to the park, allowing the crew to have maybe 15 minutes together (if that) before walking onto the field. In those situations, an "advanced pregame" that touches on the highlights that must be covered are all that the crew members may desire or have time for.

Before getting to the issue of what the elements of an advanced pregame may be, remember this: When the crew contains one or more raw rookies — and no offense to raw rookies, because everyone was a rookie at one time — or umpires new to the area or league, or the crew has not worked together much, if at all, they are shortchanging themselves and doing a disservice to the game if they take the "highlights" approach. They are not going to be on the same page when balls are hit and people are running all over the field, and bases are likely to be left uncovered with umpires calling plays long-distance. When newer umpires are in a crew, they will want a more detailed pregame, but are afraid to push the issue when confronted with a veteran partner or crew chief who doesn't want to be bothered with that. Veterans must remember what it was like to be uncertain about what to do and where to go in given situations, and to be afraid of speaking up for fear of alienating the senior umpires, and they must be willing to initiate a discussion that covers things in more detail than they are used to doing. For their part, younger officials need to be willing to risk a confrontation by asking to review things they need to know. Sometimes a gentle lead-in like, "Jon, it would sure help me out if we could spend a few minutes talking about X, Y and Z" can soften up even the most jaded and disinterested partner, and make him amenable to a constructive discussion.

What are the elements of an advanced pregame? First, here's what can be excluded, because these items should have been addressed in Umpiring 101 clinics and in more advanced clinics. They include basic starting positions in the system being worked, who has fair-foul and checked-swing responsibilities, who will stand where at the plate conference and between innings, how to handle rundowns, and how arguing balls and strikes and bench jockeying should be handled. Fights are a sufficiently rare occurrence that they can be glossed over. And everyone should know that arguments should be left one-on-one (umpire–head coach) unless they become prolonged or there is an ejection, in which case someone else needs to intervene.

Some items, on the other hand, need attention no matter how experienced the crew is or how long the members have worked together, for they will come up time and again in all games. Here are the candidates for the "advanced pregame":

RULE OR MECHANICS CHANGES

At least at the beginning of the season, it's essential to be sure that everyone is up to speed on what new rules and mechanics have been adopted since last season and how they are going to be implemented. That requires some discussion, for even if everyone in the crew has gone to the clinics like they should, the possibility of uncertainty or confusion in that area still exists, and it may not come to light if there is no dialog. Reasonable people can hear and interpret things differently, so it is necessary to get everyone singing from the same song sheet before hitting the field. As the season wears on, those items can be downplayed or dispensed with, but not at the start of the season.

NON-VERBAL SIGNALS

It's a good idea to spend a few minutes being sure that everyone will use the same signals for infield fly, standard and reverse rotation, umpire going out, appeal, time play, trap/ catch by catcher on third strike and outs and count. It's nice for each person in a given crew to know what others mean when signals are given, and the only way to ensure that is to discuss them.

It is also worth mentioning how one partner (A) may signal another (B), without drawing the attention of outsiders, if a play develops, in which B calls it, an argument ensues and A realizes he has information that B doesn't have — e.g., the fielder momentarily juggled the ball on a tag play, but B didn't see it so he called the runner out. There are now, at all levels, instances in which it is permissible for umpires to confer in the spirit of getting the play right, just as there are times in which the calling umpire must live or die with the call.

But sometimes an umpire doesn't realize that he is missing some piece of the puzzle, and the light will go on only when he sees his partner standing there with his hat off, taking a few steps toward him, or doing whatever else has been worked out so A can non-verbally tell B, "I've got information you need, but you need to ask me for it." On judgment calls, of course, (not when rules misapplications are about to occur) umpires can intrude on each other's territory only if asked to do so.

OUTFIELD COVERAGE

Nothing looks worse than having multiple eyes watching fly balls, or multiple umpires running to the outfield, leaving parts of the field visually or physically uncovered. No matter how long you have worked together, take time to talk about how you're going to divide up the outfield and infield in terms of fly ball and line drive duties. Determine who is going to be the "quarterback" that dictates who runs to the outfield, and who is going to which base when someone goes out. Remind yourselves of the need to pause, read and react instead of taking off to the outfield like you've been shot out of a cannon the instant the ball leaves the bat. Ignoring the pause, read and react formula accounts for more blown outfield and bases coverage than does a lack of understanding of who has which responsibilities.

BASE HIT COVERAGE

In some instances that dovetails with outfield coverage, because the latter will dictate the former. Whether the ball is hit in the air or on the ground to the infield or outfield, however, a crew needs to be sure that everyone understands who is going to do what with particular runner combinations, or the bases empty, and a ball is hit here or there. What are you going to do if there is no one out and a batter hits a gapper that looks like a triple? If there are runners on first and second and no one out and a fly ball is hit to deep left that may or may not be caught? If a runner on first is thrown out at third and then there is a throwback to second to get the batter-runner sliding in there? If there is a base hit with two outs and the bases loaded? When, in a three- or four-umpire crew, are you going to reverse rotate?

There are no items in a pregame that are completely expendable, but when time is an issue, there are some that can be put aside more readily than others. That is because they involve situations that rarely arise or basic mechanics that everyone should understand from day one. When you only have a few minutes to talk before a game, or you've worked together for many years and don't want to "go basic" all the time, spend your time on the situations that you know will occur in the game.

CHAPTER 02

THE MOST IMPORTANT JOB: GET THE PLAY RIGHT

In order to progress, umpires must be assertive and project decisiveness. Those attributes are commonly described as "looking good." A dilemma that many umpires face is when looking good conflicts with getting the call right. The current thinking at all levels of play is that getting the decision correct must prevail over any considerations of pride. That means that previously rendered decisions may be reversed, but that doesn't mean that any and all decisions can be changed. Let's explore the guidelines for changing calls. Except where noted, the material applies equally to NFHS, NCAA and pro rules.

Regardless of whether two- or three-umpire mechanics are used, each play is assigned to a specific umpire. In some situations two umpires may have to observe a play because responsibility for the call cannot be determined until the play is over. For example, with no runners on base, a foul popup near the first-base dugout should be observed by both the plate and first-base umpires. When the play is over, responsibility belongs to the umpire who could see the fielder's glove at the time of the catch/no catch. If both could see it, the closest umpire makes the call.

Umpires are prohibited by rule from criticizing or interfering with another umpire's decision, unless asked by the one making it. However, if there is a possible misinterpretation of a rule, it should be brought to the attention of the umpire-in-chief.

An umpire should seek help when his view is blocked or his position is such that his view of critical elements of a play *may* have been blocked. An umpire should also seek help when he has any doubt and believes a partner may have additional information that could result in getting the play right. Umpires should not seek help on plays on which they are 100 percent confident in their judgment and view of the play.

Coaches are not entitled to a second opinion when the calling umpire is certain his decision is correct. On other occasions, a coach may ask the calling umpire to "get help" on a play in which there is no possibility of another umpire changing the call. The calling umpire, as a tool to appease the coach, can go to his partner, and initiate a conversation that only he and his partner can hear. Here's an example of how that tactic might work:

B1 swings and hits a ball that goes directly down into the ground in front of the plate. While F1 fields the ball and records a routine out at first base, the third-base coach is screaming that the ball went off the batter's foot and should be ruled foul.

To calm the situation quickly, the plate umpire can go to his base umpire and say, "I know if you had the ball foul, you would have called it that way." The base umpire would be nodding his head, making it look like the plate umpire is genuinely asking for help. The plate umpire can then return and tell the coach that his partner didn't have the ball foul.

Asking for help without really asking is a tool that is effective in limited situations and should not be used frequently.

Judgment calls cannot be reversed except in very limited circumstances. Here are examples of calls that could be changed:

- Deciding if a home run is fair or foul.
- Deciding whether a batted ball left the playing field for a home run or ground-rule double.
- Cases in which a foul tip is dropped or trapped by the catcher.
- Cases in which a foul fly ball is caught or not.
- Cases in which a fair fly ball is caught or not if there are no runners on base.
- Cases in which an umpire clearly errs in judgment because he did not see a ball dropped or juggled after a tag or force.
- Cases in which a fielder may have pulled a foot.
- Spectator interference.

• Balks called by an umpire who clearly did not realize the pitcher's foot was off the rubber.

Most plays in which the sole issue is the umpire's judgment are not subject to reversal. One example is a steal play. If the issue is simply what came first, the tag or the touching of the base, there cannot be an appeal. However, if the ball is dropped without the calling umpire's knowledge, then an appeal and reversal could be in order if another umpire saw the drop. On force plays or plays at first on ground balls, there cannot be an appeal unless the ball is dropped or the foot pulled. Swipe tags could be appealed if there was an umpire with a better view. Balls and strikes, other than checked swings, cannot be appealed. Also, some calls cannot be reversed without creating larger problems. An example is a "catch/no catch" with multiple runners.

Play 1: With the bases loaded and one out, B1 hits a low line drive near the right-field line that F9 dives and catches. The plate umpire rules the ball was trapped and calls "no catch." All runners advance one base. **Ruling 1:** The simplest part of a reversal would be to declare B1 out and remove him from first base, but what about the other runners? Could R2 and/or R3 have tagged and advanced anyway? What about R1? Is it fair to put him back on first? Changing the call on that play is not possible because there is no way to fairly place the runners. That is just one of those mistakes that can't be fixed.

Here is a play in which an umpire should have offered assistance.

Play 2: With R1 on first, one out and an 0-2 count on B1, F1 inexplicably uses the windup. R1 breaks and reaches second as B1 swings at a pitch in the dirt for strike three. B1 advances to first on the dropped third strike and is safe. **Ruling 2:** B1 is out since first base was occupied at the time of the pitch. The fact that R1 had already reached second when F2 got possession of the ball is not a factor.

In the actual occurrence, the plate umpire allowed B1 to remain on first and the base umpire didn't correct the error because it wasn't his call and no one asked him. That is a clear misapplication of the rule and it is inexcusable to not get the play right.

In the following play, the call was corrected, but the lack of assertiveness on the part of the plate umpire created an awkward situation. The pitcher should not have had to appeal.

Play 3: With one out and runners on second and third, B1 hits a popup just beyond second base. F4, F6 and F8 all converge on what is clearly a trouble ball. The base umpire properly moves toward the cutout at second to make the call on the catch. F6 makes a diving catch. Meanwhile, R3 is well off third and is undecided as to which direction to run. He attempts to return to third and F6's throw beats the runner back to the base, but the tag is high and late. The base umpire improperly calls the runner safe. F1 then appeals to the base umpire that R3 had not tagged up. **Ruling 3:** After discussing the play sequence with the plate umpire and determining that R3 had never legally tagged up, the base umpire reverses his call.

When an umpire seeks help, he should do so shortly after making his original call. He should not have a lengthy discussion with the coach or others and then ask for help. If the calling umpire seeks help, he should include other umpire(s) who would likely have the best position to see the elements of the play. That conversation must take place away from players or coaches. Such meetings should be infrequent and not become a substitute for umpires seeking proper angles, exercising sound judgment and having the conviction to stay with a call that an umpire believes was properly made. Remember the ultimate decision to change a judgment call always rests with the calling umpire.

CHAPTER 03

THINGS YOU DIDN'T LEARN AT YOUR ANNUAL CLINIC

Almost all umpires, regardless of level, are required to go to some form of preseason clinic. While many of them are conducted with the greatest of care, there are simply too many umpires, with too many sets of circumstances, to cover everything that you need to make it through the season with ease. Beside the obvious things being taught at clinics, here are several things that merit further study.

PENALTIES

No doubt there was some coverage of penalties, but generally the focus tends to be on rules, not on the penalties for violations of the rules. You learn about what constitutes interference, what a balk looks like and how to get the best angle on batter's interference. There is far less time spent on what to do when those infractions occur. There is nothing worse than making a great call, only to misapply the rule and end up with egg on your face. Think about all the calls that you see in the course of the year, and then think about what awards, outs or warnings must be given when they occur. Be sure to pregame those things with partners. Umpires can also do a great service by bringing up rule enforcement situations at local association meetings so the same problems don't get repeated.

PARTNERS

When you attend your clinic, you always see new faces. More than likely, you are not provided with biographical information on those unknown umpires, but inevitably, you will be assigned to work with a few of them. In those situations, replace your normal one sentence confirmation email with a phone call (or at least a longer email). Find out a little bit about them and their past experience. If you have been around a while you might want to check to make sure they have the same uniform as you, they know where to meet and know the local rules and regulations. If you are an association newbie, get in the habit of doing that before every game.

PLACES

Every year there are always new schools, remodeled schools or fields under construction. When you have an assignment at either a new facility or a "facility in flux," make sure you know where the field is, where to park, if there is a dressing facility and if there is anything else quirky you need to know. Ask other umpires who have preceded you in going to those schools for their suggestions, or call the school's AD or the coach.

PRACTICALITY

By nature, clinics and meetings give information in the most black-and-white manner possible. That is prudent, as ambiguity leads to inconsistency. However, during the season, not everything happens in a cut-and-dried fashion. You should have a good understanding about how you are going to deal with situations that require you to "act on the fly."

For instance, if you show up at a school and find that the field is not properly marked, do you forfeit the game? Almost assuredly not. You may, however, insist that changes are made, or failing that you might have to file a report with someone. In other cases, you might just recognize circumstances that suggest the best course of action is none at all. What about your strike zone? I'm sure your clinician told you to rein in that big outside corner of yours. However, if you are working a game with that same clinician and it is 24-2 in the second inning, he might be changing his tune if you don't open it up. You need to think through those scenarios before they occur so you can deal with them easily and consistently.

PREPARATION

Preparation is not about proper hydration or remembering to wear a protective cup when doing the plate. Instead, preparation refers to the things you didn't learn at the clinic because no one can teach them to you. The late John McSherry would not speak to anyone for an hour before he did the plate; that was part of his preparation. While for most umpires, that is not practical, every umpire has little quirks that should be recognize and prepared for. For example, it is not wise to eat a heavy lunch when you have a plate job the same night. Some people also despise working plates without notice. You must diagnose your own idiosyncrasies and then find the best ways to prepare with them in mind.

Hopefully those few extra ideas will augment the things you learned in your annual clinic. Almost assuredly, however, there are other important things that have gone unmentioned. Only through working, making mistakes, missing calls and then learning from those errors will you be able to compile important tips for your own personal clinic.

CHAPTER

04

WHEN IT RAINS, BE READY BEFORE IT POURS

The toughest issue in umpiring to deal with is weather. That doesn't mean when a flood comes or lightning strikes two miles away, when just about any umpire would know to suspend play. Instead, it's referring to times when the field is just mushy enough to make it doubtful whether play should start or go on but it is not clear-cut one way or the other. With that in mind, here is a list of things to keep in mind when dealing with all of the issues surrounding weather. The decisions you make must be supported by rule, but in case rules don't cover them, remember that player safety must be the main concern. With all the lawyers lurking, do what you reasonably can to get the game in, but not at the sacrifice of safety.

FINAL CHECK OF WEATHER

Check out the forecast on your TV station or Internet so you'll have an idea of what to expect. Forecasts can be wrong, but you should be aware of what's expected in the area. If the game is supposed to start at 5 p.m. and bad weather isn't set to move in until midnight, then all is well. But if weather is supposed to hit two hours after the first pitch, you'd better know what to do when it does hit.

MEET WITH BOTH COACHES

If a weather situation is expected, get together with the home and visiting coaches when you arrive, tell them what you know about what is coming and when, and see what they know. Remember, the decision to start the game belongs to the home coach or game administration until the umpires assume jurisdiction. Only then can the crew chief make a decision to halt the game. Decisions related to weather should be the product of collaboration and agreement. Include *both* coaches. Just because the visiting coach can't make the decision, it doesn't mean that he shouldn't be involved.

SCHEDULE IMPROVISATION

If the teams are scheduled to play three games in three days
and rain is forecast for the third day, find out if they are willing
to move the third game away from the weather predictions.
Often, teams will make accommodations to get all of the
scheduled games in, even if it's not according to the original
schedule.

GROUND RULES TO COVER?

Especially with conference play, it is important to know what
the game-ending procedures are. Does the game have to be
played to its completion, or are five innings enough? Is a
halted-game rule in effect under which play can resume from
the stopping point the next day if it is necessary to stop the
game? And will the teams play each other tomorrow so that
rule can be implemented? Whether the game is final if stopped
today or can be resumed tomorrow will affect the decision-
making process in terms of whether and how quickly to stop.
In other words, be as prepared as possible in advance.

KNOW THE TEAMS' SITUATIONS

It helps to know what situation the teams are in. There may
be strategic reasons why a home team coach will want to start
a game when your best judgment counsels against it. If you
suspect that, it will make it easier to pull the plug once the
game is in your jurisdiction. Knowing the individual histories
and situations will also make the likely motives clearer when
rain persists during a game and the teams suspect that you're
approaching the point of stopping things. Teams that are ahead
in the game or have other reasons for wanting it stopped will
moan about playing in such awful conditions, whereas teams
guided by different motives will urge you to continue playing.
Ultimately, you have to understand that what the coaches are

saying is often not what they really mean — put their yapping out of your mind and do what your judgment and experience tell you must be done.

WHAT'S AVAILABLE

Find out before the game starts how much water the field holds and whether or not it drains quickly. Also, it's good to know what kind of tarp (if any), grounds crew (the home team's players?) and drying agents (such as Diamond Dry) are on hand.

If you start and a steady rain begins early, one issue involved in how long to continue will be the kind of field cover available, assuming there is one. Does it cover the infield or only the plate area and the pitcher's mound? Is it solid or does it have holes in it? Who puts it out? Where is it located? How quickly can it be gotten on the field? If the players are the crew, consider covering the field more quickly than if there is a regular crew, because you don't want to fuel a claim that a player got hurt because of sudden lightning or everyone had to hurry too fast. Also, be quicker to cover if continuing too long might cause you to "lose the field" for later games if you're in a series or tournament. Conversely, if the field cover is inadequate, consider playing on as long as possible, because covering it would accomplish little or nothing.

KEY AREAS OF THE FIELD

If the game progresses in a rain hard enough to get things pretty wet but not really to warrant stopping, pay particular attention to its effect on the mound and plate area, specifically how it affects the pitcher's striding motion and the ability of batters to get out of the box. Next check basepaths and where the infielders are stationed. Don't worry much about outfielders — even in high school and college these are kids, after all, and they like playing in slop — unless it becomes a lake, and then the condition of the mound, plate and infield is likely to be bad enough to cause you to stop. You can also ask pitchers to tell you if they feel themselves slipping, for you might not detect that. If there is a drying agent available, be pretty quick to get it out. Once you see the players start slipping, things have gone on long enough.

KNOW THE RULES

If you order the field covered, it is required by some rulebooks and customary otherwise to wait at least 30 minutes before calling the game. Again, the umpires have sole authority in that area, but it's not a bad idea to get the coaches involved in deciding whether to resume. If they can agree to stop or to try to play on, that takes you out of it, unless you think their decision is unreasonable. If they disagree, you have to decide. If you had the field covered, you probably don't want to start unless the rain has completely stopped, and for a few minutes, for it is hard to justify stopping again when you started in the rain. If a weather radar is available at the stadium or someone can access it on a laptop, check it out before deciding how to proceed.

LEGAL STALLING

In a weather situation, be ready for the gamesmanship to start. The team that is behind will start wanting to rush everything in order to catch up. Meanwhile, the team that is ahead will move at a snail's pace. The winning team may change pitchers three times in the inning and make two other defensive substitutions. And when his team is at bat, the coach with the lead might request an offensive conference and tell his batters to not swing at any pitches. It is the umpire's job to make sure the game is played within the rules. Pitching changes, substitutions and slow at-bats are not illegal. Keep the game moving at the same pace as you would if rain weren't a factor.

EVERYONE WON'T BE HAPPY

Rain situations can be very hard to deal with for veteran and new umpires alike. Simply put, they seldom leave everyone happy. If you understand and accept that, you'll have an easier time dealing with the whining and begging that you may have to endure. In the end, do as much advance planning as you can, put player safety first, try to get consensus among the competing coaches when feasible, but trust your own judgment and instincts and do what you think is right.

TOP TAKEAWAYS

Lightning Demands Respect

Judgment is required to determine when or if to stop a game due to rain or darkness. Not so with lightning. Approaching electrical storms demand immediate action.

How do you know when lightning is too close? If you can see it, it's too close!

Ninety percent of lightning discharges take place within the clouds. Those discharges merely light up the sky and never touch the ground. It's the other 10 percent that you have to worry about.

Thunder is the audible sound produced by a lightning bolt. Thus where there's thunder, there's lightning, but not all lightning produces thunder.

You can estimate the distance to lightning using the "flash to bang" method, although it has limitations. Because light travels faster than sound, you will always see the flash before you hear the bang. If you count the lag between sight and sound in seconds (1,001, 1,002, etc.) and divide by five, you'll have the approximate distance in miles between yourself and the lightning bolt. However, that computation tells you nothing about the distance between yourself and the next lightning bolt.

The danger in estimating the distance to the last strike is that it may have occurred in the farthest portion of the storm, a storm that is moving toward you. Consequently, the next strike may be a lot closer. Weather generally moves from west to east and several counts using flash to bang can be used to verify the storm is moving away.

Some stadiums have access to radar, lightning detectors or both. If neither of those is available, you will have to keep an eye on the skies to determine if it's safe to resume. Many conferences have policies regarding how long the game must be delayed if it is stopped due to lightning.

CHAPTER

05

DARKNESS, TIME LIMITS PRESENT POSSIBLE ISSUES

One of the beauties of baseball is that there is no clock. To win the game, a team must not only outscore its opponent, but also record the required number of outs on defense — most of the time.

At various levels of amateur baseball, it's common for umpires to find themselves dealing with a time limit, imposed either by a league or by Mother Nature.

Consider the following situation: Dusk is setting in as you prepare for the top of the seventh (and last) inning. The home team has a 7-2 lead.

In most amateur leagues, including NCAA and NFHS, if the visiting team takes the lead in the top of an inning and the home team does not tie the score or take the lead in the bottom half, the score reverts to what it was at the end of the last completed inning. It should be noted that both NCAA and NFHS have rules in place that potentially alter how games will end.

Absent those rules and keeping the situation above in mind, ask yourself two questions: First, what does the visiting team have to do to win (or tie) the game and second, is there enough daylight left for it to do that?

In the above scenario, the visiting team must score at least five runs, then record three defensive outs for those runs to count. Even if five batters hit home runs, that activity would require a minimum of 12-15 minutes, including time for the teams to change sides after the top of the seventh.

If you don't think there is enough light to play for another 15 minutes, you're better off calling the game immediately, rather than starting an inning and not being able to complete it.

You might get some grief from the losing manager, particularly if it's still light enough to play when you call the game, but not as much as you will if you have to stop play in the middle of the inning with the bases loaded and the tying run at the plate. There is no reason to start an inning you know you won't finish. Keeping the players on the field after a game has been decided exposes them to the risk of injury and you to possible legal jeopardy.

Simply put, if you start an inning, you're telling the teams you are going to do everything possible to finish it.

The home team's advantage in that situation can be expanded. Consider a seven-inning game with the same 7-2 score. But now the home team is coming to bat in the last of the sixth as darkness begins to fall.

For the visitors to tie or win the game they must retire the home team in the sixth, score a minimum five times in their half of the seventh and retire the home team again. If there isn't enough daylight for them to do all that, call the game right then, regardless of how bright it is at the moment.

That situation will likely get the most backlash from the manager of the team that's behind; he'll likely say something like, "It's still light" or, "They're still playing on the other field."

Explaining the hopelessness of his team's situation may require some careful wording and tact, but you should be able to convey that you had a reasonable basis for the decision.

If the score is reversed, that is, the home team is trailing, 3-1, then the outcome might be different. Why? Because it only has to score twice to tie or three times to take the lead. It doesn't have to get three outs on defense for the runs to stand up, and therefore, it doesn't need as much real time to tie or win the game.

When the rules are adjusted in NCAA or NFHS play to allow for games to be suspended, keep playing as long as daylight allows. But never allow the conditions to become hazardous to the players. If you're having trouble picking up the pitches, or more likely, if fielders are having trouble seeing line drives or fly balls, it's time to call it a night.

TIME LIMITS

Games below the varsity level often have a predetermined time limit, such as that no inning may start after two hours, or else a specified curfew.

If either of those are the case, you or your partner must keep the official time. If a two-hour rule is being used, timing should start when the first pitch is actually thrown, not when the pregame meeting ends at the plate. The players are entitled to as much of a game as you can give them.

If a curfew is in effect, make certain coaches know what time the curfew occurs and what time your watch has. That eliminates any discrepancy issues.

Even with predetermined ending times, it is important to know the game situation. If the game is in the bottom of an inning when the time limit is reached and the home team is in front, call the game at that point. It might be tempting to keep going for an extra batter or two, so the sub who just came into the game can get a turn at bat, but resist the temptation. You could be held legally responsible if you extend the game and someone is injured.

Curfew or time limit rules are also frequent in adult recreational leagues. Those leagues usually stipulate that no inning may start after a certain time, such as three hours for a nine-inning game.

Many of the same principles that apply at other levels are then in play. Be sure both teams are aware of the time limit and know the league rules on extra innings if the score is tied when the time limit hits.

In all cases, keep in mind your job is to umpire the game. Do not intentionally short players at any level on time when there is a reasonable chance that the next inning can be played.

CHAPTER

06

TEAMWORK IN UMPIRING

In his book *The 17 Indisputable Laws of Teamwork*, John Maxwell describes and explains the importance of teamwork in organizations, families and athletic teams. While all of the "Laws" are critical and appropriate to those groups, some are particularly important when being applied to baseball umpires. Let's look at a few of the most significant and how umpires can become better through the implementation of the Laws.

Not all sports officials, at all levels, work an entire season together or advance as a unit, so let's pay particular attention to Maxwell's wisdom on being a better teammate or partner. Most umpires are selected and assigned as individual officials and advance in their careers or to postseason assignments as such.

However, teamwork is imperative to success and to a successfully officiated game. Maxwell notes that, "One is too small of a number to achieve greatness." That certainly is true in officiating. Umpires cannot be successful and or work a great game by themselves. The athletes are too fast, the coaches are too demanding and frankly, no one is that good. Umpires need partners, and the higher the level the game, the better the partners needed. Baseball umpires need to be strong individually (balls and strikes, fairs and fouls) but also must be strong as a crew. They need help covering third base in a rotation situation. They need for the first-base umpire to move to the outfield to cover that close home run versus foul ball, and they need for the plate umpire to handle a difficult coach in the dugout.

Accepting the above as a given, what are the traits of a good teammate or partner? It should start with good communication well before the game. While a crew chief should initiate contact about any travel issues and game time confirmation, a strong partner will not sit and wait and cause a potential problem if the crew chief does not take the initiative. Umpires must be proactive, professional and be prepared long before arriving at the game site. How committed are you to communicating with the other members of your crew? Are you supportive of everyone, even the people who aren't your friends? Are you holding a grudge against anyone on the crew? Are you jealous of their success? If you are, you need to clear the air. If there are any barriers to good communication standing between you and another crew member, you need to remove them. That is your responsibility.

Another trait of a good partner is the ability to sometimes assume a lesser role. Have you ever been in a game in which your past history with a coach is only a detriment? Can you step aside and let your partner, (possibly a younger, less experienced official) handle a situation that your history or personality would only escalate? You must think of the good of the crew and the game and not only or your "position," "role" or "status" on a crew.

In Maxwell's fifth law (The Law of the Chain), he writes, "Most people's natural inclination is to judge themselves according to their best qualities while they measure others by their worst."

How true is that in officiating? Most officials constantly compare themselves to others, especially those who are getting the "better" games. Maxwell adds, "As a result, they point to areas where their teammates need to grow. But the truth is that every person is responsible for his own growth first." Are you as demanding of your own work as you are of your partners? Do you constantly look to the weaknesses of others while promoting yourself? Do you engage in a meaningful postgame analysis of your work? Do you constantly pick apart the work of others and place blame instead of accepting your position and responsibility in your crew?

In Maxwell's sixth law (The Law of the Catalyst), he discusses how to become a stronger team member. Those thoughts can be adapted to the officiating world. Maxwell asks, "How are you when it comes to crunch time? Do you want the ball, or would you rather it was in someone else's hands? ... If you avoid the spotlight because you are afraid or because you haven't worked as hard as you should to improve yourself, then you need to change your mind-set."

That mind-set is prevalent in officiating and must be corrected to ensure quality officiating and good teamwork. Younger or less experienced officials must not shy away from difficult situations or immediately look to another crewmate to intervene. If you find yourself with that mind-set, try these two things:

FIND A MENTOR

Officials become stronger only with the help of officials who are better then themselves. Find someone who steps up in difficult situations and have that individual help you grow into that role.

GET OUT OF YOUR COMFORT LEVEL

You won't know what you are capable of until you try to go beyond what you've done before. In other words, step up. Try experimenting a little in lower-level assignments. Become that leader, that take-charge official whom others look to in tough situations. Learn from your mistakes and keep applying yourself to improve and be a better crewmate in all your games.

Whatever your level of experience, first-year umpire or Division I College World Series veteran, you can improve your commitment to being a good crewmate. Communicating, adapting, self-evaluating and stepping up are just a few of the ways that you can adapt Maxwell's book to officiating.

CHAPTER 07

MOVING UP THE ASSIGNMENT LADDER

At the 2007 NASO Summit, prominent NCAA Division I men's basketball official Ed Hightower related a story about how first- and second-year officials weren't happy working their way up the ladder. They expected to be immediately selected to work conference tournaments and even put into the later stages of the NCAA tournament.

Everyone knows that's just not going to happen in any sport. Some umpires will advance through the ranks quicker than others and some never will.

With those thoughts in mind, here is a list of the things that have been successful for umpires moving up in college baseball. And while the main focus is at the collegiate level, these tips apply no matter what level you are currently working and what level you aspire to work.

GO TO SELECTED CAMPS

There are a ton of camps to go to, however you must do your research to make sure the camp is the right fit for you and you are the right fit for the camp. You want to try and go to camps that are geographically located where you want to work. If you are from the Midwest, you would want to go to a camp where there are going to be umpires present that work in conferences in the Midwest or the assigner of those conferences will be observing.

Many times conference coordinators will take recommendations from veteran staff members. You are not going to be able to absorb everything that is taught to you at a camp, and you are going to get many different philosophies. Take a few things from each camp that you like and try to implement those things into your overall approach to umpiring.

WORK EVERY GAME LIKE THERE IS SOMEONE WATCHING

Whatever level you are working, you need to give a complete effort with proper enthusiasm. Umpiring is a privilege, and you should work every game as if it is the most important game in your career. Whether it is a Division I conference game or a non-conference junior college game, you never know who is watching in the stands or what coach is respected by the conference supervisor.

LISTEN TO THE VETERANS

Most veteran umpires will not have a problem with someone asking them the path they took to get to where they are. Those are guys who have been fortunate enough to get to an elite level of college baseball as umpires. When a veteran umpire is talking and taking the time to answer a question, "be all ears."

FIND A MENTOR

If you have someone in your area that is an established umpire and you like the way he works, try to model yourself after that umpire. That will take a bit of work because not only do you want to look at the umpire as a role model on the field but off the field as well. Pay attention to the way the umpire handles coaches, carries himself with a purpose and his mechanics. Also, watch the way the umpire acts in the locker room, the way he comes dressed to the field, how he treats game administration. Umpiring at the higher levels is not about balls and strikes or outs and safes. Instead it is about game management and the "off the field" behaviors.

DON'T PUT THE CART BEFORE THE HORSE

Going back to the story that Hightower relayed, it might be
cliché, but there is also a great deal of truth to that statement.
Umpires cannot expect to make a jump to Division I when they
are only working small college ball currently. But how can you
know when you are ready to make the next step? A great rule
of thumb is once you have worked a conference tournament
or regional at the level you are currently working, you are
ready to make the next step to a higher level. Many careers
have gotten shattered when guys try to rush up the ladder too
quickly and get thrown into the fire. The next thing you know,
they are on the scratch lists and the advancement dreams come
to a screeching halt.

ADVANCE CORRECTLY

If you are offered a game in a level above what you normally
work, and you are serious about moving up, take the game.
However, if you have a previous assignment for that day, check
with your current assigner and explain to him the situation
before you commit to the game you were offered. By asking to
get removed from your current assignment to work up a level,
it shows your assigner that you do care about the game that he
had offered to you. Most of the time, those opportunities come
at the last minute and you will have to travel more than you
are used to. However, it will show that you are a team player
and willing to make the commitment to work at a higher level.
Whatever level you want to get to, it will require sacrifices.

CHAPTER 08

CASE STUDY: EXAMINING A SAFETY SQUEEZE BUNT

There is a cliché about "big things coming in small packages." Baseball's version of that might be that "a lot of big things can happen on the smallest of plays."

During a summer game played under NFHS rules, the following play happened with a runner on third and no outs. The right-handed batter laid down a bunt, the runner (who was not breaking on the play) scored and the batter was thrown out at first.

At first glance, that looks like a pretty routine play. However, it was far from that.

THE BUNT

The batter did an excellent job of catching the ball with the bat, deadening the ball. In fact, the bunt did not leave the dirt circle around the plate. That led to several instant decisions that had to be made.

First, was the bunt fair or foul? The bunt stayed fair, but since it wasn't outside the dirt circle, it was the catcher who attempted to field the ball, making it harder to read the exact moment he touched the ball and leading to another potential situation.

THE CATCHER AND THE BATTER

Even with a runner on third, the catcher moved from behind the plate to field the ball. That immediately raised the possibility of interference. In fact, there were two possible types.

The first was between the catcher and the batter. The catcher has the right to field the ball without interference, while the batter has the right to run to first base without being obstructed. As long as neither one does anything intentional and both players were doing what they were supposed to do, they could have made contact and nothing would have been called.

The second potential interference was the batter touching the ball. With any bunt that remains in the dirt circle or along the first-base line, the plate umpire must make sure that the batter-runner does not kick or get hit by the ball. If he does, then he is out and the ball is dead.

In the play, there was no interference so the play continued.

PITCHER, R3 HEADED HOME

Because the catcher moved to field the ball, the runner had an easy decision on the safety squeeze — he broke for home. Defensively, the pitcher headed toward the plate in case the catcher wanted to attempt a throw.

Those two decisions raised more calling possibilities. The most obvious was if the catcher did indeed field the ball and attempt to shovel it backward.

That didn't happen, but what did occur was the pitcher's momentum carrying him to and beyond the plate without the ball. Fortunately, he clearly beat the runner there and got out of the way, so there was no obstruction or malicious contact from either side.

PLAY AT FIRST BASE

The run has scored; all that's left is the routine play at first. Only the way the entire play developed, routine isn't going to happen.

The batter-runner is headed toward first base and is more than halfway there. He's also completely in fair territory. There is no doubt he's headed toward running-lane interference. Fortunately, the first baseman and catcher react and the throw goes to the outside half of the bag. The first baseman is able to catch the throw cleanly (which is the main criteria for interference) and the batter-runner is called out.

A simple sacrifice bunt, scoring a runner from third. If only the actual play had been that easy.

CHAPTER 09

WORKING THE PLATE: MUCH MORE THAN JUST BALLS AND STRIKES

A head coach for a high school team who was a former Division I college umpire once said that if he was going to have one good umpire and one lesser-qualified umpire (by his standards) on a game, he would rather have the good umpire on the bases. His reasoning was that even the best umpires will miss pitches during games, but that plays on the bases involve safes and outs, and he wanted to see those plays called by the better umpire.

While that theory worked for him, a good plate umpire has many more responsibilities before and during a game than just calling pitches.

BEFORE THE GAME

There are several tasks that must be completed before the plate umpire even puts the ball into play:

Pregame conference. Generally speaking, the plate umpire is the only umpire who should talk during the meeting. After reviewing the lineup of each team, the plate umpire must verify that each team is legally and properly equipped. An answer of "Yes" is required, not just a nod. At that point, the home coach gives ground rules, but if there are any concerns, generally about safety, the plate umpire may overrule.

PITCHES

While this article isn't talking about calling pitches, there are several points the plate umpire needs to keep in mind:

Strike three mechanic. Most plate umpires enjoy calling strike three. The problem occurs when their strike three mechanic (or dance steps) takes them out of the action. A plate umpire should be careful not to turn away from the playing action with runners on base. If the batter interferes with the catcher on a stolen base attempt, the plate umpire must see that.

Batter's box rule. That rule came into effect to eliminate unnecessary delays during a batter's plate appearance between pitches. It is the responsibility of the plate umpire to enforce the rule, using the common-sense guideline of why the rule was created. A good umpiring technique is to tell the batter to get back into the box, and only penalize batters who refuse to get back in or continue to cause delays.

PLAYS NOT AT THE PLATE

In the two-umpire system, the plate umpire is responsible for many happenings outside of the clay circle at home. Here are just a few:

Base umpire goes out. The plate umpire must read his partner's actions on fly balls to right and right-center field. Either way, the plate umpire should already be out from behind the plate, because he will have to rule on the fly ball if the base umpire does not take the ball. If the base umpire goes out, the plate umpire has the batter-runner touching all bases.

Force-play slide rules. Both NFHS and NCAA rules require that runners going to a base on a force play slide or get out of the way of future plays. Since the base umpire will most likely be turning away from the play before any interference occurs, it is the plate umpire's responsibility to make this call.

With only one runner (going into second base), the plate umpire should move to the left side of the diamond and try to get near the pitcher's mound in order to see the action at second base.

Remember, the rule was written as a safety rule, not an interference rule. The plate umpire must make the call for any violations, regardless of whether the runner actually interferes with the play. If that call is made, the batter-runner is also out and all other runners return to the base occupied at the time of the pitch.

Running-lane interference. If the batter-runner is running outside the three-foot lane and interferes with the attempt to catch a good throw, the plate umpire must be in position to rule on that play. The plate umpire should not reward bad throws, but the throw doesn't have to hit the runner for interference to occur.

Swipe tags and pulled foot. On a routine ground ball with no runners on base, the plate umpire should strive to reach the 45-foot line that starts the running lane. That will put him into the best position to watch for swipe tags or if the first baseman pulls his foot off the base. If your partner asks for help, answer his question and let him make the call.

Rundowns. If there is only a single runner on base and a rundown ensues, the plate umpire should be able to assist the base umpire. The plate umpire should go to the corner base (first or third) and move into position while the play is going away from him. The plate umpire should then tell his partner that he is in position to assist. Also, any rundown between third and home is primarily the plate umpire's call, and the base umpire should move into the third-base cutout if there are no other runners for which he is responsible.

Rotations. With a runner on first only, or with runners on first and third only, the plate umpire is responsible for plays at third base involving R1. If the ball is hit into the outfield, the plate umpire should head to third in foul territory and only move into the third-base cutout if the ball and runner start to converge at third. The plate umpire must verbally communicate to his partner that he is at third, otherwise the base umpire is still responsible for that runner.

With runners on first and second only and fewer than two outs, the plate umpire is also responsible for the runner going to third base on a tag-up when a fly ball is caught in the outfield. If the fly ball is caught, the base umpire has the tag-up at second, but the plate umpire should have rotated to third in the same manner as above and be ready to make a call at third base.

PLAYS AT THE PLATE

Plays at the plate are often the most exciting that occur in a game. The plate umpire must be in good position for the plays, which are usually very close. He must also be aware of all the possibilities that can occur during those plays:

Where to start. The plate umpire should be just off the clay circle, behind the plate and lined up with the point of the plate. That starting position enables the plate umpire to move toward either the first- or third-base line extended to get the proper angle for the throw as it arrives.

Establish a good angle. The umpire should let the throw take him one or two steps in either direction from his starting point. Once a tag has occurred, make the catcher show the ball before making a call.

Sacrifice flies inside the "V." In that case, the base umpire has the catch, so the plate umpire's responsibility is to line up the tag with the catch. Often, that will take him very near the third-base dugout. Once the catch is made, the plate umpire can get back to the plate area quickly enough to make a call.

Sacrifice flies down either line. In that case, the plate umpire must remember his priorities. Fair-foul and catch-no catch come before either the tag at third or the play at the plate. The plate umpire should never take fly balls to the outfield by backing up behind home plate. And if the fly ball is deep, the plate umpire must go up the line as far as possible. The deeper the fly ball, the less likely there will be a close play at home. See the catch and glance to make sure the runner tagged up.

Time plays. If there are two outs, the plate umpire must be aware of tag and appeal plays that happen at other bases. The plate umpire should line himself up behind the plate along with the base where the play is being made. The base umpire should not rush his call, because the plate umpire should have seen when the tag occurred. If the base umpire calls the out, the plate umpire then either scores or waves off the run.

CHAPTER

YOU'VE GOT TO HUSTLE, BUT WHAT DOES THAT MEAN?

Hustle is a term that is commonly used in umpiring, but rarely defined. Dictionaries offer at least a dozen definitions of hustle. The one most relevant to umpiring is to move energetically. But hustle in umpiring is much more than that. It is actually a state of mind as much as it is a physical act. Genuine hustle may best be defined as a dedicated and enthusiastic commitment to fulfilling complete game responsibilities. Here is a look at five forms of hustle.

FUNCTIONAL HUSTLE

In the words of *Successful Sports Officiating*, "Hustling is an intense dedication to being in the right position from which to view a play." Proper hustle may be the one ingredient that separates good umpires from mediocre ones.

Getting to the proper spot in a timely manner allows an umpire to see the whole play. That is essential in order to make an accurate judgment. An umpire cannot accurately make a safe/out call on a tag play if he's not able to see between the players as the runner slides into the fielder. That is especially true when the tag is applied above the runner's foot. The umpire must determine if the glove touched the runner's body before the runner's foot touched the base. Only a proper position will give the umpire the requisite angle.

Getting to the right position requires a good start. The base umpire must immediately recognize the possibility of a trouble ball (converging fielders, near a foul line, etc.) and begin his movement before he actually determines it is a trouble ball and will not be a routine play.

A good start must usually be followed by a sprint, especially when the game action to be seen is relatively far away, such as a hard line drive to an outfielder. In other situations, it could also mean running under control, a lope or a trot.

FALSE HUSTLE

Officials must be wary of "false hustle" — energetic movement during live-ball coverage that serves no purpose other than to demonstrate the official can move rapidly. The real problem with false hustle is no officiating is accomplished while the official is showing how fast he can run. One example is the base umpire who, with no runners, takes the batter-runner to third on an extra base hit and moves so fast that he doesn't get a good look at the runner touching second base.

Closely related to false hustling is hurrying. Many clinicians will use the phrase "hustle, don't hurry." That term is often not explained and the official is left to figure it out himself. Consequently, the phrase can be more confusing than helpful. Hurrying is impulsive behavior — rushing when there's no need for either making a rapid judgment or getting to a particular place. It can also be excessive or extraneous movement, or simply overzealous decision making. The distinction between hustle and hurry is best explained through examples.

An umpire hurries when he calls the play before it happens. While some calls can be changed, other calls, such as that of a foul ball, cannot. There is no advantage to hurrying a call.

OVERHUSTLE

It is possible to hustle more than is necessary. Doing so can result in reduced coverage when the official overruns the optimal position from which to observe his responsible area.

On a sacrifice bunt, an umpire can overhustle by getting into position for the wrong base. Fielders don't always throw to where they have the easiest play. Another example is making the pivot from the A position so quickly that the touching of first base is not observed. Overhustling with a wide pivot leaves the umpire out of position if there is a throw back to first.

DEMONSTRATIVE HUSTLE

Unlike false hustle, the so-called demonstrative hustle does not detract from the game, but unlike functional hustle, it doesn't really contribute to making calls. What it does is contribute to officiating by creating the perception the official is actively doing his best.

Demonstrative hustle includes the base umpire moving from his position on the foul line to his position in the infield after a batter receives a base on balls and moving to his position from the infield to short right field when an inning ends. The plate umpire can show he is a hustler by moving sharply back to his position behind the plate whenever he returns there.

MENTAL HUSTLE

The state-of-mind concept means thinking deeply and perceptively throughout the game. Part of that is "keeping your head in the game." The baseball umpire exhibits mental hustle by knowing where the runners are, the number of outs and the ball/strike count (without looking at his indicator).

Another aspect of mental hustle is anticipating the play. Anticipatory behavior is a form of hustle. It is applying knowledge to expected behavior and getting ready to reach a position almost before a play ever takes place.

Baseball umpires who have their head in the game will anticipate steals, squeeze plays and sacrifice bunts as well as runners who will try to take an extra base.

Hustle is both show and substance. It is also both a behavior and an act of will. A hustling official actively works the game and does not sit back and react or loaf through it. He avoids coasting and is perceived as an energetic contributor. Aside from being called blind, the next most damning thing an umpire can be called is lackadaisical, refusing to hustle.

CHAPTER

ANTICIPATE, THEN REACT

Anticipation. Is it a dirty word in umpiring or a necessary facet of the craft of a skilled umpire?

There is no question that you can get in trouble if you anticipate what the call will be on a judgment play before it happens. Catch/no catch, fair/foul, safe/out, and ball/strike calls should be made with an approach that is not biased to what an umpire thinks might happen given the circumstances leading up to the play.

Have you ever had what you and everyone else expected to be an easy out at first on a bunt or a comebacker to the pitcher, only to have the fielder throw a bad lob to first, turning it into a bang-bang play? It never helps your judgment on a play when your self-talk says, "That guy is a dead duck" just prior to having to rule on a play.

However, anticipation plays a very important role in the mind of a quality umpire, when that anticipation involves foreseeing where the next play might be.

That is especially true in two-umpire mechanics, where all initial and subsequent plays have to be covered by only two umpires. In a classic double-play situation, the base umpire can't afford to get too close to the play at second when he has to be in position to rule on the succeeding play at first base.

However, in the same situation, a seasoned umpire may be able to tell when only one play will result at second or first on a ground ball fielded by an infielder. That umpire will be able to get a little closer to the only play that will result. That will mean being in better position to see a very tight play or at least demonstrate the appearance of being in the best possible position to rule.

A common maxim in umpiring is to always keep your eyes on the ball and glance at the runners. Keeping that simple tenet in mind can go a long way toward helping you anticipate where the next play will develop.

Knowing the speed of the runners in various situations can also help with the anticipation of where the next play might be.

A very fast runner may be more likely to try to stretch a single into a double, or take an extra base on a hit by one of his teammates. In two-umpire mechanics, when the plate umpire rotates to third for a play, he can't get too close, especially with a faster runner going into third. There is always the chance for an overthrow or a misplay by the fielder covering third that may result in a play at the plate. Very few umpires will win a race with a player to the next base.

Another situation in two-umpire mechanics in which anticipation is key is when a pickoff throw to first catches the runner by surprise, and he starts toward second to avoid being tagged out by the first baseman.

With no other runners on base, a plate umpire who is on the ball will anticipate that there will be a rundown and will hustle up to first to cover the back side of that possible rundown.

That could also happen with a runner at second only, where a pickoff move creates a possible rundown between second and third. If he can get to third in time, a good plate umpire will be able to split the coverage with his partner.

One area in three-umpire mechanics in which sometimes anticipation is not properly taken into consideration is on a base hit with a runner at first base or first and third base. When the runner at first commits to third on the base hit, P will rotate to third and U1 will rotate to home. U3 has got to anticipate the possibility of a throw back to first base on the batter-runner and slide over toward first for that possibility. Some umpires miss that possibility, and can be caught off guard and way out of position when it happens.

Perhaps the ultimate anticipation play for umpires to be aware of is the time play. Many circumstances arise in games that will create the possibility of a time play at home, where an umpire must determine if the runner scored before the third out was made on the bases. Among those circumstances is any two-out situation in which a base hit happens with a runner at first, second or with the bases loaded. Also, tag-up time-play situations can happen with only one out and runners at second and third or with the bases loaded. Anticipating a close time play at the plate will require the plate umpire to be in great position to see both the runner scoring and the third out being made on the bases.

One final area that anticipation can come in handy is when something unsportsmanlike has happened that might lead to retaliation by the offended team.

When an umpire sees a player gesture to the opposing dugout after hitting a home run, or stand at the plate and watch for a few seconds before going into his home run trot, awareness tells the seasoned umpire that you may have a knockdown pitch coming the next time that batter hits.

Anticipating that type of retaliation can allow you to warn the catcher of the offended team not to engage in that kind of behavior. If that doesn't forestall the expected retaliation, at least you will be in a state of mind to issue warnings immediately in an attempt to calm down what, unchecked, could become a volatile situation.

Anticipate the play, not the call, and your game should go more smoothly.

CHAPTER 12

THE BEST THING TO SAY: SOMETHING CLOSE TO NOTHING

Anyone who has ever given a deposition in a legal proceeding was probably advised by his lawyer to do two things: Think before you talk, and say as little as possible. Lawyers know that depositions can be traps for the unwary, for the questions you are asked will be asked again if the matter goes to trial a year or so later. Opposing counsel is hoping you'll say something that, at trial, can let him make you look evasive, inconsistent or otherwise lacking in credibility in the eyes of the judge or jury. The more you say, and the more you stutter, backtrack and repeat yourself, the more rope you create to hang yourself with later on.

Although the parallel between giving a deposition and umpiring a baseball game may not be readily apparent, there is one.

To put it bluntly, too many umpires have a tendency to want to explain themselves, sometimes endlessly, when it would be better to find a muzzle. The less you say, and the more carefully you say it, the better off you are.

Let's start with the plate conference. There are some subjects that, per the rules at each level, you are required to delve into. Under NCAA rules, for example, you must ask the coaches to certify that their bats and helmets comply with applicable standards. And under NFHS rules, umpires must ask if all players are properly and legally equipped and confirm that all bats and helmets are legal.

At the first of the year, moreover, bring up new rules that you want to be sure the coaches know about and ask them if they have questions about rule changes. Coaches may not have even read about the changes, but ask anyway. That way, if something happens during the game that requires you to invoke a new rule, it's hard for them to say that you are pulling something out of the woodwork or that they didn't know what's going on. They'll probably say that anyway, but it's easy to reply, "Coach, we gave you the chance at the plate conference to ask about new rules."

Be careful not to hold a rules clinic at the plate conference. Coaches don't want to hear it, and the more you go on and on about this or that rule, new or old, the more they will get antsy and their eyes will glaze over. Worse, the umpire who prattles on endlessly creates the perception that he is one of those hyper-technical umpires that coaches cannot abide. The reality, of course, may be that the umpire is trying to engage in preventive umpiring by raising issues so as to avert problems later on. Admirable goal, but as has often been said, the negative perception thus created will be far more important than the reality. For that reason, carefully pick and choose what subjects you raise, discuss them in layman's terms without citing the applicable rule or quoting it chapter and verse, and quickly move on.

The same philosophy applies when going over the ground rules. First, generally ask the home coach to do it. It's his yard, and it saves him having to correct you if you make a mistake. More important, he now controls the conversation. If he wants to expound at length, that's his prerogative, but he can't blame you for it. If you don't understand something or want to make some observation, chime in, but otherwise it's his show and keep quiet.

Take the same approach in arguments and when you need to make a point about something. Say you call a balk on a pitcher for not coming to a complete stop in his stretch and the coach comes out to protest. Some umpires in that situation say things like, "Coach, rule nine says a pitcher must come to a discernible stop. That was a point of emphasis at the NCAA clinic. Your pitcher's leg was coming up while he was bringing his hands down in front of him. That's not a discernible stop." What's wrong with that? One, the coach couldn't care less whether rule nine or rule 909 is the pitching rule, so that is lost on him. Two, quoting rules by number makes you sound like a hyper-technical umpire. Three, "discernible" is the correct word, but it comes across as one of those five-cent words that can make you look like you think you're a stud buzzard when you use it. Four, the coach could also not care less that it was a focal point at this year's NCAA clinic; to raise that issue, moreover, makes it look like you were sitting on dead ready just waiting to pull the trigger and enforce the rule. Five, the discourse is too long and repetitive. Six, the overall tone of the comments makes it sound like you're lecturing the coach, which is a real turnoff. And that's for starters.

What could you say? "Coach, he didn't come to a complete stop." If he wants to prolong the discussion, as he probably will, mention the leg coming up before the hands settled, because that is relevant information that he needs to know, but that's all that needs to be said. If he wants to keep going, say, "Coach, I told you what I had. There's nothing else to say." After awhile he'll run out of gas and you can move on. What you cannot do is allow yourself to get into a wordy, repetitive, back-and-forth. That will prolong the discussion past the point of reasonableness, because he'll feel compelled to respond, etc. It also raises the possibility that you might say something that appears to contradict something you said earlier, which really gives him something to get on you about, or that you'll inadvertently say something out of line that he can go to your supervisor to complain about.

Same thing if you are getting grief from the dugout on balls and strikes. We've probably heard umpires say things like, "Gentlemen, I've heard enough on balls and strikes. If it doesn't get real quiet I'm going to start at the far end of the dugout and work my way forward throwing people out until the yapping stops." Or, "One more word and someone is going," which will inevitably prompt someone to say, "Word."

Better to avoid the dissertation and threats and just say, "That's your ball-strike warning." There is no need to say anything else. That covers the necessary territory without threats or embellishment.

As has been noted in many other clinics and columns, it is important, when arguments arise, not to feel compelled to get in either the first or the last word. That is part of the deposition advice. You are far more likely to keep those discussions shorter and focused on the precise issue at hand if you keep quiet and let the coach clarify his objection before you say anything. If he's ranting, say nothing. Most people run out of steam when ranting after about 20 seconds so let him wind down, and then you can talk. By keeping quiet and making sure you understand what he's complaining about — you may think it's X when it's really Y — you make it look like you are listening to him, which is what coaches want, and you give yourself a chance to compose what you want to say so that it's short, accurate and to the point, without any unnecessary words. The quicker you talk, the more likely you are to say the wrong thing, start sputtering, ramble or become repetitive. None of that creates the impression that you are on top of things.

There are times when you cannot keep completely quiet and when one-word answers won't do because more information needs to be conveyed. You don't want to come across as uncommunicative, curt or abrasive. As a general rule, if you take a moment to compose your thoughts, keep what you say as concise as it can be, and steer clear of rule references, high-falutin' words and extraneous information, what you say will be much more effective and well-received.

CHAPTER

HIT THE ROAD, COACH (AND DON'T COME BACK NO MORE)

Not much excites a crowd more than a coach-umpire argument, especially when they really get after it by going nose-to-nose with their jaws flapping and fingers pointing at each other. Things reach a fever pitch when the umpire steps back, throws his arm over his head and gives the coach the heave-ho. Good theater? You bet. However, when an umpire has to resort to the death penalty, doing it calmly is better, for that way he looks like he is in control of himself and is not getting caught up in the heat of the moment. Image is everything, especially in this day and age. It is important in terms of game control that the umpire looks like he is above the fray and in command of the circumstances and himself.

Some will disagree with some of what is said here. There are those who believe there is nothing wrong with an animated ejection, and that it is difficult to keep from doing it when we're being called every name in the book. Others will say that a lot of umpires are too easy and willing to look the other way and avoid problems. Ignore what you can, avoid confrontations if you can. Those rules have worked for a long time and are what the following suggestions are based upon.

If an umpire gains a reputation of being firm and in command but reasonable and not a red-ass, he'll acquire respect and have to eject fewer people over the long haul. You don't earn respect by being trigger happy and acting as if you're looking for trouble. You may make people fearful, but that's not the same as respect. If you keep your voice (and the rest of you) under control, even when you are being challenged about a call — you don't yell and scream, don't threaten people and tell them to shut up, and eject them at the drop of a hat — they'll pay attention when you do get worked up about something because it's out of character.

Over the years there have been umpires who have skyrocketed down the ladder because they became so aggressive and confrontational that people felt they couldn't talk to them. Supervisors definitely get more calls from coaches and administrators about that kind of umpire more than someone whose judgment they think stinks. Getting that reputation is probably one of the quickest ways to buy a ticket out of the higher levels of ball, or to keep from getting there. It's a killer, and once you have it, it's almost impossible to overcome.

As for when to eject someone, there are magic words that should guarantee a quick exit, with no warning. Anything derogatory preceded by "You" fits the bill. Saying, "You made a h-------- call" is one thing; saying "You're h--------" is something else. Goodbye. And the former will also buy an exit if the speaker persists. In that case, tell him something like, "You've made your point. No more," and if you hear it again, goodbye. Coaches and players know that, although some will try to act like they don't.

One question that has been asked a lot is how to handle a batter who draws a line in the dirt with his bat to signify that the pitch was off the plate. There are different theories on that. Some umpires say, "You've just drawn your strike zone for the rest of the day." Famous longtime minor league umpire Tom Ravashiere once took the bat and extended the line, put an arrow at the end, and told the batter to follow it to the dressing room. The former gets you into the threat realm, for while the coach and player both know he was wrong, you give them ammunition to use against you when you make comments of that sort. The latter is the type of showmanship that no administrator would buy today, as funny as it may be.

The simple answer is to tell the batter to hit the road. No showmanship or big wind-up ejection, just a statement. Trust me, he knows what the deal is, and if he doesn't, well, what a fine educational experience he just had. That's showing you up, and no umpire has to tolerate that; in fact, if you don't take care of business, you'll get the reputation of being a doormat and others will think you're fair game from then on.

When you're getting static from the dugout on balls and

strikes, don't jerk off the mask and bolt in that direction with the, "One more word ..." comment. Now you've invaded their territory, and when you go back to the plate you're certain to hear a rejoinder. (Players have been known to shout out "word" — goodbye.) Look over there, put up your hand, and say firmly, "I heard you. Enough." That usually does it, but if the music continues, stop, take out your lineup card, tell them, "That's your ball-strike warning." Make a production out of it, so everyone in the park knows that a warning has been issued; after that, if they persist and you run them — and since you warned them, you'd better — it's harder to fault you. And again, no big wind-up. They're less likely to come charging out of the dugout and do the chest-to-chest routine if you give them a mellow ejection signal than if you look like a gymnast. If you know who's talking, direct it to him; if you don't, direct it to the head coach. Few things are as calculated to make a coach take control of his players than warning him when you don't know who the culprit is. Another option is to look for tennis shoes — a player, for example, who pitched yesterday and isn't going to today — and run him. That makes the point but in a non-harmful way.

It doesn't hurt to unobtrusively signal that a pitch was out or in if you get, "Where was it?" from the dugout. Once or twice, that is — more than that is too much — and depending on who's asking, do it if the coach is reasonable, but if he's a jackass, don't because he'll just use it against you. And don't signal players if they ask. Keep your hand at your chest and motion slightly in or out so that the crowd can't see it. That sends the message that you're approachable and don't think you can't miss one. They generally respond well to that. Of course, if you do that and they hit you with, "No way," or something similar, the deal's off. That's when you can say, "What the heck did you ask for? Don't ask again 'cause I'm not answering."

If the pitcher comes off the mound or raises his arms or

otherwise visually conveys his displeasure, don't storm out there, because then you look like the aggressor. AL umpire Terry Cooney did that in the 1990 AL playoffs when Roger Clemens showed him up, and afterward everyone forgot about Clemens' antics and crucified Cooney. It's not right, but it's a fact — the players and coaches can throw fits, but if you look like you're going after them, you get the bad rap. Tell the catcher to go out and tell the pitcher to knock off the Academy Award performance or he's done for the day. Or call the coach out and tell him that the next time it happens, goodbye.

Got a catcher holding pitches or catching balls and moving them back in the zone to buy a strike call? Walk around, dust off the plate and tell him, so the crowd doesn't know what's going on, that the next time he does that, he's through. That way you take care of business without anyone else being the wiser.

If you have a close call on the bases and a runner or fielder is upset, don't stand there admiring your fine call and signal. Walk away. That way they have to come after you, and then they look like the aggressor; some will even give up and leave. If they get animated, tell them to stop waving their arms and calm down and then you can talk, but not until then. If they're heated, do what former NL umpire Doug Harvey used to do — look them straight in the eye and say nothing for 20 seconds. Eventually they will run out of gas because the average coach or player can't string more than 20 seconds of words together. When they calm down, you can say, "Now, do you want to listen to me?" Usually you can have a conversation, let them get rid of their steam and go on.

If you call a hitter out on strikes and he has to walk toward the first-base dugout, take a step toward the third-base dugout. Vice versa if he goes the other way. If he comes after you, he looks like the aggressor and you look like you were trying to avoid a problem. If he makes some throwaway comment under his breath, like, "Pitch was outside," ignore it the first time as long as he doesn't visually show you up or get in your face, but instead keeps walking. If there's a second comment, say, "That's enough — I heard you the first time." If he persists, run him, but now he ran himself and everyone knows it.

If a coach tries to bring up a play that happened last week or earlier in the game, head him off at the pass. In fact, say, "Coach, this isn't a history class. I don't want to hear about what happened before. If you want to talk about this play, fine; otherwise, the conversation's done." If he persists, walk away; if he continues, warn him; if that doesn't do it, goodbye. If an umpire ejects someone, his partner(s) need to intervene and get the offender away. The ejecting umpire needs to clear the scene. Not easy when the adrenaline is flowing. Get between him and your partner and ease him away.

There's a fine line between letting too much go and being trigger-happy, and each umpire has to figure out for himself where to draw it; in fact, one reason that it's a bad idea to try to move up the ladder too quickly is that you don't learn where to draw the line overnight. It takes a lot of games dealing with a lot of different situations and personalities to learn how to be between a doormat and a red-ass. Baseball is not like other sports in that there is no intermediate penalty such as 15 yards or a technical foul; it's either ejection or nothing, so you need to be sure it's warranted when you do it.

Today, what the powers-that-be want at all amateur levels — and increasingly in the pro ranks — is for you to be communicative and approachable and to avoid confrontations if you can. However, when all else fails, take care of business.

CHAPTER

STRETCHING THE LIMITS: BASEBALL'S ELASTIC CLAUSE

Of all the major sports, baseball is probably the one most prone
to events that do not have direct rules coverage. Retired AL
umpire Jim Evans agrees that baseball seems to have more of
those opportunities than any other sport. He also believes that
umpires will not always find adequate explanations to help
rectify problems when an umpire has erred.

In the early days of the game, the rulemakers took a
wait-and-see approach. When something out of the ordinary
occurred, the umpire would do whatever he thought was fair
and rules would later be changed to address the situation.
One example is the rule regarding interference at the plate by
a retired runner, which emanated from an umpire's on-the-
spot decision in an 1887 American Association game. On an
infield grounder that was booted, a runner scored from third
and the runner on second tried to score. R3 hung around the
plate and seeing his teammate would be out, he shoved the
catcher, preventing a tag. In the melee that followed, the runner
on first also scored. However, umpire Wesley Curry declared,
"Obstruction," called R2 out and disallowed R1's run —
baseball had a new rule.

Surprisingly, the "elastic clause" which gives umpires,
especially the umpire-in-chief, authority to rule on situations
that are not covered by rule, did not appear in pro rules until
1953.

Evans sees a clear need for an elastic clause rule to enable
the umpire to make a ruling on the spot that fairly administers
the "spirit of the rules." Evans said, "Those 'on the spot' rulings
should be made with common sense and in the best interest of
fair play. It is critical that the umpire has a thorough working
knowledge of the rulebook so that he does not create a ruling
that is already covered in the book."

The NFHS and NCAA agree such a powerful rule must be
used carefully. The rule does not allow rules to be created or
ignored at an umpire's whim. It is not intended for umpires to
set aside book rules for what they'd prefer. The rule can only

be applied to those points that are not covered in the book. "An umpire must not only know what is in the rule book but he must also know what is not in the book," Evans said. "Otherwise, he might make a ruling that contradicts an existing rule."

During Evans' professional career, he encountered the elastic clause every two or three years. Those odd happenings were usually put into the interpretation manual the following year, but not every play or situation that occurred found its way into the official rules.

According to Evans, an example of a situation in which the elastic clause would apply is the rule stipulation of the penalty of a one-base award when a player uses detached equipment to touch a pitched ball. There has always been a provision for a batted ball (three bases) and a thrown ball (two bases), but no provision for a pitched ball. When they encountered that situation, umpires invoked the elastic clause and awarded one base. After that, it was explained in the interpretation manual, but did not make it into the rulebook until years later.

A glaring misuse of the elastic clause, for example, would be to award three bases for a batted ball that goes beyond a very deep fence. "He would have easily had a triple," claimed the prep umpire who actually did that several years ago.

A rare use of the elastic clause at the major league level was made in a game between Cleveland and Baltimore several years ago. In the top of the third inning, with runners on first and third and one out, Baltimore's Ramon Hernandez sent a liner to center field. Grady Sizemore made a sprawling catch and threw to first to get Miguel Tejada for the inning-ending double play. Before Tejada was put out, however, Nick Markakis tagged up and scored from third.

The run should have counted. The play was a time play and not a force play. However, plate umpire Marvin Hudson waved the run off without protest from the Baltimore bench. In the bottom of the sixth, crew chief Ed Montague called the press box and told the official scorer to give Baltimore another run. Montague's decision gave Baltimore a 3-2 lead in a game it eventually won, 7-4.

Although the decision to count the run did not affect the outcome of the game, the Indians contended that Baltimore lost its chance to get the run back when it did not protest the cancellation of Markakis' run before Erik Bedard threw his first pitch in the bottom of the third inning.

Montague's report of the incident made it clear that the umpires corrected the mistake in the interest of "getting it right" without an inquiry from the Orioles. In fact, that situation is not an appeal play, but simply the correction of an error. MLB's statement said, "Mindful of (the umpires') obligation that the first requisite is to get decisions correctly, as the rules instruct them, this umpire crew was within the authority that Rule 9.01 (c) gave them to correct the game score when they did."

The umpires were not covered by the "next pitch" rule, since there is no rule that states an umpire's mistake must be corrected by the next pitch. That is an example of how 9.01 (c) can be correctly used.

Sometimes situations occur and umpires would like to use the "elastic clause" to cover up a mistake, but that's not proper. Take an example from a playoff game in Colorado in which an unusual situation occurred due to a different type of umpire error.

The three-umpire crew was assigned to a field it had not worked before and none of the umpires walked the perimeter to familiarize themselves with the field. The outfield fence was a single fence that varied in height. At the right-field foul pole, the fence was four-feet high and in right center it abruptly rose to eight feet to protect a tennis court.

From the plate area, the eight-foot portion could conceivably be viewed as two fences. Since it was only one fence, a batted ball has to clear the fence to be a home run.

Any ball hitting the fence remains in play. That was discussed as part of the ground rules in the pregame conference. However, the first-base umpire apparently misunderstood the explanation.

And of course, it came into play. With a runner on first, a batted ball hit just under the top of the highest fence and bounced back. The home team's right fielder knew the ball was in play and reacted accordingly. The first-base umpire, who correctly went out to observe the "trouble" ball, signaled home run. Both R1 and the batter-runner saw that home run signal and began to trot. The ball was relayed home and R1 was tagged out after a rundown between home and third. The batter-runner ended up on third.

The umpires conferred and decided to let the out stand. Most surprisingly, no one was ejected. The exact discussion that took place is unknown, but the first-base umpire later stated, "I signaled the home run, but did not kill the ball."

The umpires could have applied the rule that allows umpires to rectify their own mistakes when a runner is placed in jeopardy, but chose not to do so. Since there is rule coverage for fixing an umpire's mistake, the elastic clause would not apply. Because the rule does not state how a situation should be rectified specifically, one could argue that the elastic clause would be used in making the base awards.

CHAPTER 15

TAKE CARE OF BUSINESS

Situations often arise in ballgames when a gentle touch by an umpire can go a long way toward defusing things.

By that, it means to do something in a quiet, unobtrusive manner so as to "nip a problem in the bud," as Barney Fife used to say on the old *Andy Griffith Show*, without the average spectator even recognizing it.

Developing that touch and knowing when and how to apply it are not things that umpires learn overnight. That is one of the many reasons that that it is necessary to pay your dues and take things a step at a time in climbing the ladder.

Umpires who advance too quickly may be "book smart" — know the rulebook inside and out and the nuances of the Deep C position — but they will likely lack the "street smarts" that one can only learn by going around the block a few times.

It's important to be a history student before the game. As much as you can, find out about what kind of relationship the teams have had in the past. If you regularly work in the area you'll probably know that, but maybe not, and if you are working two teams from out of your area, you may be caught off guard by something that happens.

Has there been bad blood between the teams? Repeatedly? Do the coaches not like each other? Is there some school district/location/region issue involved? When things happen — fights or near-fights, beanball incidents, excessive chirping — that your fellow umpires need to know about, because they will have those teams the next day or somewhere down the line, it's incumbent on you to pass that information along to the supervisor/assigner and to the next crew itself, if possible. Otherwise a pitch that seemed to innocently slip out of a pitcher's hand and go behind a hitter might have really been a "purpose" pitch.

ARRIVAL AT THE SITE

Before the game, it's important for the umpires to let the home
coach know when they've arrived at the site. Nothing more
than going to the fence, getting his attention and giving a quick
wave of the hand is needed, but it reassures him that the crew
is there and that things will get started on time.

Pitchers, especially at higher levels, have a set routine
they like to follow in warming up and they want to know the
game will start on time so they can begin warming up at the
appropriate time.

When a coach assumes the umpires are on hand but they're
running late due to traffic or cutting it close getting off work,
the game will start late and the starting pitcher will warm up
only to have to stop, cool off and then start again. That can be
more than a minor irritant that can carry over to the field.

KEEP IT BUSINESSLIKE WHEN YOU WALK TO THE PLATE

Problems can arise when you stop to chat with players and
coaches, especially the home team's, because the visiting coach,
especially if he doesn't know you, will notice that familiarity.
Everyone knows that coaches are paranoid, and they won't
say anything to you about it — how can they, without risking
ticking you off? — but they'll file it away in their memory bank
and maybe use it against you if a funky play happens.

Coaches can form impressions of umpires with whom
they're not familiar by watching their body language as they
walk to the plate. Either they convey the impression that
they're ready for prime time or they don't, and those first
impressions can last forever.

THE PLATE CONFERENCE

In the plate conference, cover what needs to be covered — or
let the home coach review the ground rules if he prefers — but

keep it short. Not too much jocularity, and especially the off-color kind, because you never know when a coach you think is "one of the guys" is a deacon in his church who's offended by that sort of thing.

Don't make it a mini-rules session. Depending on the new rules, you can if they have questions about changes, but don't view the plate conference as a time to have a seminar.

THE START OF THE GAME

To start the game, some umpires make a big point of carefully dusting off the black edges of the plate, and then some. Especially if players and teams don't know you, it can convey the message that you intend to call a big strike zone. It's hard for a hitter approaching the plate to start the game to see you making a big production of that and not understand the message you're sending: "I like the corners, so swing the bat." They'll also go back and let their buds know what they saw.

DEVELOP A GOOD RELATIONSHIP WITH YOUR CATCHERS

Lots of things have been written about that, because umpires have different viewpoints on the subject. It's a good idea to get their first names and give them yours, and to ask at the start whether his pitcher throws anything unusual that might surprise you.

But don't do a lot of excessive talking during the game. Both the umpire and the catcher have jobs to do and too much chatter can be distracting.

That goes for infielders as well. It's easy to want to chat with a first or third baseman if you're on the foul line or the middle infielders if you're there, and a little is OK, but don't overdo it. Certainly, you've had more than one player let you know directly or by the way he interacted — looking ahead and talking without moving his lips — that his coach didn't want him talking with umpires. If you insist on doing that in spite of the obvious clues, you can buy a lot of trouble.

PREVENTIVE MEDICINE

If you know your catcher and trust him, you can use him to send messages to the pitcher. The pitcher, for example, may be getting borderline in terms of balking — not really coming to a full stop but not really being deceptive either — so you can send your catcher out to him to tell him to give you a better stop. A base umpire can do the same thing with an infielder. Be careful, of course, in terms of who you're dealing with, because it can be embarrassing when a player gets halfway to the mound and turns around and asks you, "What did you want me to tell him again?"

In college and pro ball, and in a lot of high school games, the coaches are mature enough, and appreciative enough of the "preventive medicine" approach, that they're not likely to say anything when you give the opposition a word to the wise in that manner. They know you'll extend them the same courtesy.

In the lower levels it can be different, for often the coaches haven't been around that long themselves and see everything in black-and-white, don't-give-them-any-help terms. If they say something to you, just tell them that you'll do the same thing for them.

Sometimes things happen in games that have to be handled openly and aggressively, like calling an interference, balk or obstruction. But at times there are little, maybe unnoticed, seemingly innocent things that you can do that can avert real problems later on. One mark of a top-notch umpire is knowing those techniques and when to apply them.

CHAPTER 16

GOOD TIMING IS EVERYTHING

One umpire tells a story about timing being the first thing that he learned when he started umpiring. Keeping it as his number-one concern has allowed him to become a solid "balls-and-strikes" umpire.

The first lesson on timing might surprise you. He was asked if he had ever seen the slapstick comedy, *The Naked Gun.* In the film the main character inadvertently becomes the plate umpire for an important MLB game (remember, it's a comedy). After the first pitch is thrown, it takes the "umpire" a full four to five seconds to realize his task, and everyone waits patiently for him to ring up a pitch that is right down the middle. By the third pitch of the at bat, the "umpire" has gone from one extreme to the next, ringing up the unsuspecting batter before the pitch ever reaches the plate. The sequence is good for a laugh, but there is a great lesson to learn: If your timing is bad, you stand to look not like an umpire, but instead like a character from an oddball comedy.

So armed with that theatrical umpiring lesson, here are some tips that you can use when you are struggling to get pitches right.

BACK TO BASICS

At the first sign of trouble, immediately simplify your stance and mechanics. Then focus hard on timing. Each time you do that, you will immediately see results. As you gain more experience, you will have fewer lapses in timing, but they still happen. When they do, try to evaluate what you are doing differently and get back to basics.

SEE THE BALL INTO THE GLOVE

Everyone has seen those umpires who call pitches too quickly. Fastballs may not provide much of a problem, but breaking balls routinely can create an embarrassing moment. The ball starts at the batter's shoulders and is just breaking into the zone when a loud "ball" echoes through the stands. A few pitches later, the ball starts right at the belt and is just diving down into the dirt when that loud "strike" call makes its way around the field. If you see the ball into the glove, you can't call the pitch until it has landed in the catcher's mitt and if that happens, you have a much better chance of getting the pitch right.

PAUSE

Most umpires are taught early on that a pitch is a strike unless you have been given a reason to think otherwise. If you see the ball into the glove, pause a second and you still haven't found a reason to call a ball, then you have a strike. If at some point your mind is changed, then call a ball. But if you end up calling a strike, you should have had a full second to make up your mind.

STAND UP AND CALL THE PITCH

Another piece of good advice is to make your verbal strike call at the instant that you give your visual indication. That gives you even more time to react and look sure of what you're doing. If you call the strike before you give the signal, your timing is actually not as good as what you think it is and you are likely to miss more pitches.

Following those steps should prove helpful, but there is one pitfall that you must be aware of. While you are striving to have great timing, the players, coaches and fans are not concerned with your technique. You are going to consistently hear reaction to the pitch before you get a chance to call it. It might be a comment like "Leave that down" from the bench of the team that is at bat, or a cheer from the bench of the team that is pitching. You will sometimes even have the batter start heading down to first on a pitch he thinks is ball four, but you are about to call strike two. You should not penalize those reactions as they are almost always just that, reactions, and are not meant to show you up.

What you should also not do is be deterred by any of those actions. Call the pitch as you see it, and don't let the umpire in the dugout, coaching box or the bleachers decide for you.

Timing is critical in just about every aspect of umpiring, but it is of supreme importance while calling pitches. Watch those great "balls and strikes" umpires and you will likely see that borne out again and again. If you train yourself to be deliberate, you will likely see a fast improvement in your plate work. If you still need help, you might want to check out that scene from *The Naked Gun*; even if it doesn't help you improve, you should still get a good laugh.

CHAPTER

THE SEVEN SINS OF UMPIRING

Professional golf instructor Jim McLean often discusses a handful of "death moves" that one can make in swinging a club that can produce a butchered shot. He has never implied that they are the only possible candidates, for any golfer knows that there are many other things that one can do wrong; instead, those are his "biggies." Similarly, there are some "death moves" in the world of umpiring.

ASSIGNMENTS

One really good way to shaft yourself with assigners and supervisors is to repeatedly turn back games. Younger umpires especially must realize that umpires who do that get branded and that it can have a long-standing, far-reaching negative impact on their current and future umpiring situations. Come tournament time, or in conversations with folks who can help one advance, no assigner is going to want to help such a person. At the other end of the scale, umpires have been rewarded if they are willing to go anywhere, anytime and never give assignments back by putting them in tournaments.

PARTNERS

Always support your partner. There is way too much jealousy, backstabbing and inappropriate self-promotion in umpiring. There's no excuse to be the guy who throws his partner under the bus ("Coach, it's his call, not mine," etc.), especially when he's trying to save his own skin on a blown call or mechanic, or the guy who tries to get in a coach's good graces by agreeing when he's yanking his chain about a partner's real or perceived missed call.

In the same category are umpires who are overly friendly with players or coaches — particularly one team's — provide makeup calls, favor one team over the other, badmouth other umpires behind their backs, or kiss up to supervisors.

To get the reputation of someone to whom those labels apply can be a very harmful career move.

APPEARANCE

Without dwelling on it or repeating a bunch of information from the past, suffice it to say that how an umpire looks is a very big deal with most people. Beards and bushy mustaches and shaggy hair, looking unkempt and unshaven, being overweight, loafing on the field, having a uniform that doesn't fit or hasn't been washed since the turn of the century, refusing to wear the prescribed uniform — all are royal turnoffs to coaches, observers, etc., for they convey the message that the person lacks pride in himself and doesn't give a flip. Often, moreover, the umpire doesn't even realize that he might have killed his chances at moving up the ladder or getting playoffs or better assignments because a power-that-be happened to see him in that condition and reacted very negatively to it. Such things can also cause umpires to not get the benefit of the doubt when they make onfield calls.

PREPARATION

You can't just begin to work your schedule starting with the big games later in the season. That would do a disservice to the teams and your partners, to say nothing of yourself. Beginning the conference season so ill-prepared is something that is not fathomable. Related sins include not keeping abreast of, and properly implementing, rule and mechanic changes, not attending clinics and not working preseason scrimmages. When veteran umpires blow those things off, moreover, what sort of message do the younger folks get?

RULES APPLICATION

Generally speaking, an umpire who always enforces rules according to their literal letter is a bad umpire. Anyone who has been involved in the writing of rules will attest that even the greatest wordsmith cannot come up with language that will cover every conceivable situation and that instances will arise in which a literal application of the rule is not warranted. Top-notch, well-regarded and much-in-demand officials get that way in part because they have learned how to apply rules in light of their intent and when to ignore nitpicky infractions that have no effect on the game and put neither team at an unfair disadvantage.

GAME MANAGEMENT

Typically, younger umpires are either too officious and domineering in controlling a game or, conversely, are doormats who let everyone run all over them — constantly coming on the field to complain about everything, incessantly chirping from the dugout, etc. It takes awhile to learn how to find a happy medium where one takes charge and even gets tough when necessary but is always professional in doing so and otherwise pretty much stays in the background and lets the game run itself. Umpires have to control games at all times, but with time and proper training, they can learn to do that in almost all instances without throwing people out of games, barking commands, issuing ultimatums, and being the center of attention.

PERSPECTIVE

If you become so wrapped up in officiating, you can lose your perspective in terms of what is important in the broad scheme of things. There are umpires who spend a lot of time officiating — working football, baseball and basketball, often five and six nights a week.

Don't be surprised if your wife or partner gets frustrated and asks if that is what your plan is for the rest of your life — go from one sport to the next, etc., and never have time to go out with friends and generally kick back. As much as you enjoy officiating, make time for other things and people in your life. For almost everyone, umpiring is an avocation. It is an important source of self-satisfaction, relationships and even monetary reward, but it needs to be kept in its place. In the end, friends and family are far more meaningful than what games or tournaments you do or do not get, who else got what, etc.

CHAPTER

LET'S TALK ABOUT IT

You've just finished a tension-filled plate job and retired to the dressing room. You're ecstatic because you feel you only missed one or two pitches and no one squawked the whole game. Your partners are thrilled because both had some whackers, got them right and it was like church for them as well. As a result, several minutes are consumed with everyone patting themselves and each other on the back. Then people shower and leave.

Understandable? Sure. When things go well on the field, the natural temptation in the postgame, wind-down phase is to enjoy everything to the max. No matter how long you have been umpiring, you can probably feel the tension drain from your body after concentrating fully for three hours or more.

You want to celebrate when the game pretty much worked itself. Conversely, when the game seems like World War III, with lots of questionable and even missed pitches and plays and continuous barking from everyone, it is tempting to do nothing afterward but unload on those who gave you grief. The problem is that while both reactions are, to a point, understandable, even necessary, neither is productive in terms of improving your work.

Much has been written about the need for an effective pregame meeting. What gets short shrift, however, is the postgame phase. Although it can be easy to just break out the champagne or gripe about complaining players or coaches, depending on how things went, you also need to spend time discussing what you did well and could have done better. And there will always be things that need improvement, even in games that go well. Although people's eyes sometimes roll when someone suggests a postgame critique, because we're tired and just want to relax and blow off steam, right after the game ends is when everything — good and bad — is fresh on your minds. If you wait until later to have a debriefing, you will likely forget (or "misremember") some important events. If you never have that session, you will miss a chance to improve your individual and collective performances.

Human nature being what it is, it is easier for that kind of discussion to begin naturally when the crew members know each other well and have worked together many times. In that scenario, no one needs to be responsible for initiating the postgame critique because one person or the other always starts the ball rolling.

You may adjust the tone of what gets said if you are dealing with someone who gets his feathers ruffled a little more quickly than others, or a young umpire who could go in the tank if he gets hit too hard with criticism, but you should always end up having the kind of open and frank appraisal of what you did not — and did — do well that is essential if we're to improve. Sometimes that discussion will end up going on for a half hour or more, perhaps even spilling over to the local watering hole. On occasion, voices may even get raised.

When the crew members don't know each other well or may not have worked together much, if at all, someone will have to take the lead in initiating the discussion. If an observer is on hand and comes into the dressing room afterward, he or she will almost certainly do that. If there is no observer, the crew chief should start the dialogue; if there is no chief, the senior member should take the lead. If you're a younger umpire and no one else has initiated a discussion, do so yourself by saying something like, "Can we spend a few minutes talking about some things that happened during the game?" You may get shot down by a veteran or crew chief who doesn't want to be bothered, but the chances are far better that the result will be some kind of dialogue — maybe not as productive as you'd like it to be, but better than nothing. Then remember that when you get some years under your belt and become a crew chief or senior umpire.

Here are some suggested ground rules for postgame chats.

Observers/supervisors must be honest, but they need to be careful not to come across as condescending or too high and mighty. We've all dealt with a few whose body language, tone, etc., made it clear that they thought they became the Almighty when they donned the supervisor hat. Same with crew chiefs and senior umpires. In contrast, those who are perceived as down to earth and genuinely trying to help will get a much better reception from rookies and veterans alike.

Also, if an observer thinks the crew or some member(s) made a lot of mistakes, he shouldn't bring up each one; concentrate on the big ones, because too much criticism can beat someone down. Finally, mix in some positive comments. If the conversation ends on a positive note, the person receiving a critique is more likely to accept it because it wasn't entirely negative.

For their part, umpires can dig a deep hole if they always have a comeback for an observer's comment. It gets old talking to who always has an explanation of why he did something a certain way — he comes across as defensive and unreceptive to what was being offered. The best approach is to say something like, "Thanks. That makes sense," or, "Thanks. I'll think about that," and leave it at that. You may think that what the observer said is stupid, but don't let on that you think that. Be open to criticism, for it just may be that the observer knows how to do something better than you do.

Also, don't put your partners or assigner/observer/supervisor on the spot by waltzing in after the game and announcing that you didn't miss a pitch. If you did that great a job, the others will tell you; if you didn't, it makes it tougher on them to say anything. Not impossible, however.

The postgame critique should be comprehensive. Don't focus on one play; do a run-through on mechanics, rotations, positioning, timing, etc., throughout the game. Having to honestly evaluate oneself is tough, but one of the most constructive methods of improvement there is.

Everything suggested has been based on the assumption that, after the game, the crew will retire to a dressing facility. What if there isn't one? There are a lot of umpires who still dress in parking lots out of their car trunks. In that situation, if it's possible to have a debriefing afterward, while the crew members are taking off their gear, do so. But due to many circumstances, including irate fans, that may not be feasible. In that event, there should be some communication between or among the crew members by phone, email, etc., the next day. It's too easy in this Internet age to have some kind of multi-party exchange for there to be any excuse not to have it.

It has often been said — when the time comes that you don't want to continue to improve your work, you should quit. An open and honest postgame review of your individual and collective performance is one of the best improvement tools, so don't ignore it.

The National Association of Sports Officials

More than 18,000 of the most dedicated and devoted officials already have. They chose to join the only nationwide organization that supports and protects them year-round no matter what sport they work, and no matter what level. Now is your chance to connect with the leader in sports officiating and support your fellow officials across the nation.

RECEIVE THESE BENEFITS:

- The nation's best officiating liability insurance
- 12 months of *Referee* magazine - #1 publication of its kind
- Free sport quizzes
- Members-only print and online newsletters

- Marriott Athletic VIP card – hotel savings up to 50% year-round
- Honig's Whistle Stop 10% discount on select purchases
- Discounts on educational materials and rental cars
- Instant proof of insurance available
- And much more!

FOR MORE INFO OR TO JOIN | www.naso.org/bookjoin or call 1-800-733-6100

Notes

Notes